Tape noted
5/02

W YORK IN 1776

ROBERT QUACKENBUSH

POP! GOES THE WEASEL
and YANKEE DOODLE

J. B. LIPPINCOTT COMPANY/ PHILADELPHIA & NEW YORK

FOR PIET

who was born in New York
and likes everything about it —
especially its people and playgrounds

U.S. Library of Congress Cataloging in Publication Data. Quackenbush, Robert M.   Pop! goes the weasel and Yankee Doodle: New York City in 1776 and today with songs and pictures. SUMMARY: Illustrates two popular songs of the Revolutionary era and describes historical sites in New York City and their significance. [1. Songs. 2. New York (City)—History—Revolution, 1775-1783] I. Title.   PZ8.3.Q2Pr [E] 75-28312 ISBN-0-397-31675-5

A NOTE

In 1776, soon after the American colonies declared their independence, New York City was invaded by the British. In the years that followed, New York was occupied longer and suffered more than any other city during the Revolutionary War. For his eighth picture–song book of Americana for children, Robert Quackenbush has combined two of our oldest favorite songs to tell the story of the American Revolution in New York City.

"Pop! Goes the Weasel" and "Yankee Doodle" both originated in England and became popular on both sides of the Atlantic. "Pop! Goes the Weasel" was a singing-dancing game in which verses were invented to satirize events of the time. The familiar refrain was probably a commentary on hard times, when it was necessary to "pop" (pawn) one's "weasel" (originally a tool used by hatmakers; hence, the tools of one's trade) in order to survive. New verses have been written to the tune, telling the story of the British siege of New York as it might have been told in song at the time.

The British probably sang "Yankee Doodle" to poke fun at the American rebels, but the song was quickly adopted by the Americans, who enjoyed the humor of it. The version presented here is the one that was first enjoyed by the American patriots and that has been sung by American children for two hundred years.

The historical illustrations in this book are based on originals in the Museum of the City of New York and the New York Public Library. The views of modern New York were rendered on location.

ON JULY 9, 1776, NEW YORKERS IN REVOLT PULLED DOWN THE STATUE OF KING GEORGE III AT BOWLING GREEN

All around the British marched,
Their laws seemed harsh and evil;
Our independence we declared —
Pop! goes the weasel.

New York suffered far much more
Than other cities in the war,
Till we got to freedom's door —
Pop! goes the weasel.

BOWLING GREEN PARK TODAY

IN AUGUST, 1776, 130 BRITISH SHIPS WITH 32,000 SOLDIERS WERE IN THE HARBOR, READY TO ATTACK NEW YORK

Britain's king sent men-of-war
To stop all the upheaval;
In New York Harbor they were placed —
Pop! goes the weasel.

New York suffered far much more
Than other cities in the war,
Till we got to freedom's door —
Pop! goes the weasel.

NEW YORK HARBOR TODAY

BY THE END OF AUGUST, 1776, HUNDREDS HAD FLED NEW YORK FOR WESTCHESTER, MILES NORTH

Away from New York City fled
The panic-stricken people;
Many thought the end had come —
Pop! goes the weasel.

New York suffered far much more
Than other cities in the war,
Till we got to freedom's door —
Pop! goes the weasel.

NEW YORK CITY TRAFFIC TODAY

The Battle of Long Island lost,
Our troops left in the drizzle,
Crossed the river to New York —
Pop! goes the weasel.

New York suffered far much more
Than other cities in the war,
Till we got to freedom's door —
Pop! goes the weasel.

A VIEW TODAY OF THE SITE OF WASHINGTON'S EAST RIVER CROSSING

All around Manhattan Isle
The British fired their missiles,
Hoping they could take New York —
Pop! goes the weasel.

New York suffered far much more
Than other cities in the war,
Till we got to freedom's door —
Pop! goes the weasel.

SNIFFEN COURT MEWS, A STREET SCENE TODAY IN NEW YORK'S MURRAY HILL DISTRICT

ON SEPTEMBER 16, 1776, WASHINGTON WON A VICTORY AT THE BATTLE OF HARLEM HEIGHTS, BUT HE WAS FORCED OUT OF NEW YORK BY NOVEMBER

We held out against the foe,
Our troops were few and feeble;
We won a fight but lost the town —
Pop! goes the weasel.

New York suffered far much more
Than other cities in the war,
Till we got to freedom's door —
Pop! goes the weasel.

A VIEW TODAY NEAR 120TH STREET AND RIVERSIDE DRIVE, WHERE THE BATTLE OF HARLEM HEIGHTS TOOK PLACE

ON SEPTEMBER 21, 1776, A GREAT FIRE SWEPT ACROSS NEW YORK, BURNING TRINITY CHURCH ON THE WAY

Then New York was set aflame,
The Redcoats watched it sizzle;
Their prize destroyed before their eyes —
Pop! goes the weasel.

New York suffered far much more
Than other cities in the war,
Till we got to freedom's door —
Pop! goes the weasel.

TRINITY CHURCH ON WALL STREET TODAY

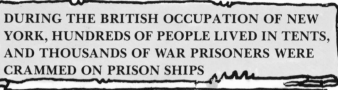

Some who stayed behind were left
In poverty most dismal;
But some had gold to see them through —
Pop! goes the weasel.

New York suffered far much more
Than other cities in the war,
Till we got to freedom's door —
Pop! goes the weasel.

HOMES AND APARTMENTS ON NEW YORK'S UPPER EAST SIDE TODAY

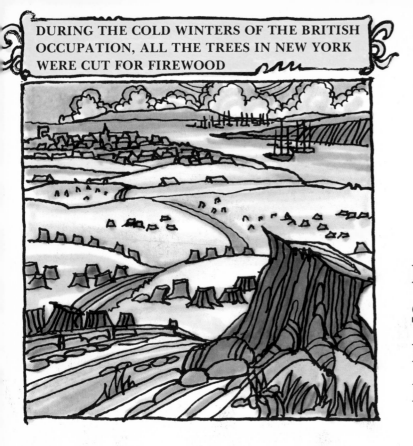

People needed firewood,
So all the trees were leveled;
New York became a barren plain —
Pop! goes the weasel.

New York suffered far much more
Than other cities in the war,
Till we got to freedom's door —
Pop! goes the weasel.

TREE-LINED PATHS IN NEW YORK'S CENTRAL PARK TODAY

FOR SEVEN YEARS THE BRITISH HELD NEW YORK CAPTIVE. THEN IN 1783 A DIFFERENT SONG WAS

HEARD AS THE AMERICANS MARCHED INTO NEW YORK AT McGOWN'S PASS AND FREED THE CITY

ON NOVEMBER 25, 1783, WASHINGTON AND HIS VICTORIOUS ARMY PARADED THROUGH THE STREETS OF NEW YORK

Yankee Doodle came to town
Riding on a pony;
He put a feather in his hat,
And called it macaroni.

Yankee Doodle, keep it up,
Yankee Doodle Dandy;
Mind the music and the step,
And with the girls be handy.

NEW YORK'S STEUBEN DAY PARADE TODAY, HONORING GENERAL VON STEUBEN, WASHINGTON'S TRUSTED ADVISER

ON DECEMBER 4, 1783, WASHINGTON SAID FAREWELL TO HIS OFFICERS AT FRAUNCES TAVERN. THE WAR WAS OVER

Yankee Doodle is the tune
That we all delight in;
It suits for feasts, it suits for fun,
And just as well for fightin'.

Yankee Doodle, keep it up,
Yankee Doodle Dandy;
Mind the music and the step,
And with the girls be handy.

FRAUNCES TAVERN TODAY

POP! GOES THE WEASEL

All a-round the Brit-ish marched, Their laws seemed harsh and e—vil; Our in-de-pen-dence we de-clared— Pop! goes the wea-sel.

Chorus

New York suf-fered far much more Than oth-er cit-ies in the war, Till we got to free-dom's door. Pop! goes the wea-sel.

1 BATTERY PARK. Protected by a battery of guns during the Revolution, the tip of Manhattan was later extended by landfill to form today's park. Take a ferry from here to Staten Island or to the Statue of Liberty and view New York Harbor.

2 BOWLING GREEN PARK. In 1786 the area where New Yorkers had bowled for over fifty years became the city's first public park. It is still enclosed by the iron fence put up in 1771 to protect the statue of King George III.

3 TRINITY CHURCH. Built on Wall Street in 1697, the church was destroyed in the fire of 1776. The present church was built on the same site in 1846. In the churchyard are buried prominent men, among them Alexander Hamilton.

4 ST. PAUL'S CHAPEL. Dating from 1766, St. Paul's survived the fire of 1776 and is the oldest church in New York City. George Washington worshiped here, as did the British officers who occupied New York during the Revolutionary War.

5 CITY HALL PARK. Liberty poles were erected here on the City Common, symbolizing the Patriot Cause. On July 9, 1776, the people of New York assembled here with Washington and his army to hear the Declaration of Independence read aloud.

6 BROOKLYN BRIDGE. If you take the boardwalk in the center of the bridge, you will follow the route that Washington and his army took when their boats crossed to Manhattan from the western end of Long Island, now called Brooklyn.

7 SOUTH STREET SEAPORT MUSEUM. Several blocks of the waterfront district surrounding the museum at 203 Front Street, which features maritime exhibits, are being painstakingly restored. Historic ships are docked here.

8 FRAUNCES TAVERN. Built in 1719 and later restored, the building at 54 Pearl Street — the city's oldest — houses Revolutionary War exhibits. In the Long Room on the second floor, George Washington said farewell to his officers.

9 FEDERAL HALL NATIONAL MEMORIAL. At 26 Wall Street, the building is on the site of the old Federal Hall where George Washington took the oath of office as the nation's first President in 1789. The museum here is open daily.

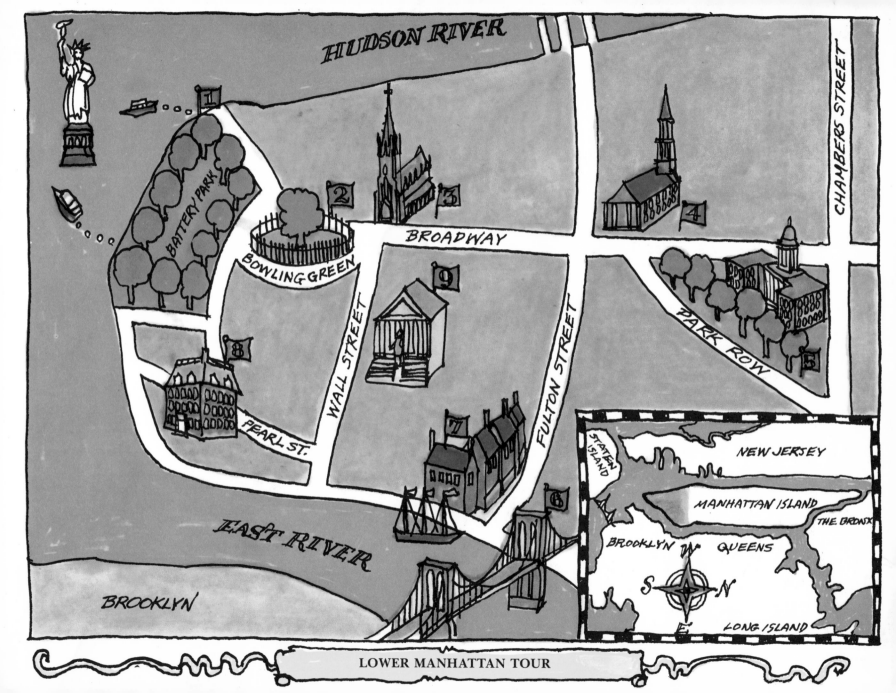

HUDSON RIVER

CHAMBERS STREET

BATTERY PARK

BROADWAY

BOWLING GREEN

WALL STREET

FULTON STREET

PARK ROW

PEARL ST.

EAST RIVER

BROOKLYN

STATEN ISLAND

NEW JERSEY

MANHATTAN ISLAND

THE BRONX

BROOKLYN

QUEENS

LONG ISLAND

LOWER MANHATTAN TOUR

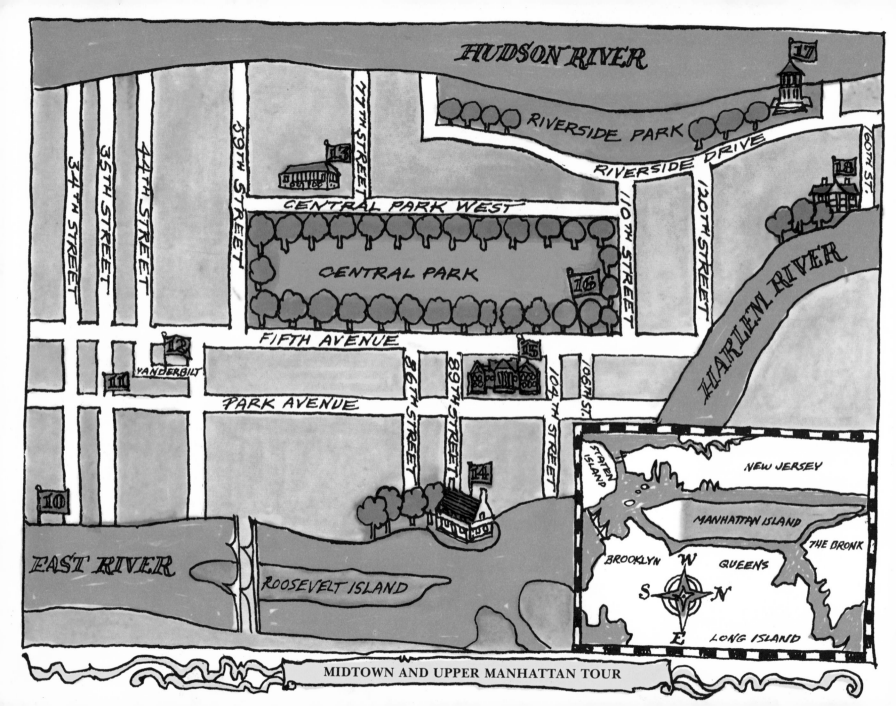

HUDSON RIVER

RIVERSIDE PARK

17

RIVERSIDE DRIVE

77TH STREET

59TH STREET

110TH STREET

120TH STREET

160TH ST.

13

CENTRAL PARK WEST

CENTRAL PARK

16

18

HARLEM RIVER

FIFTH AVENUE

12

15

VANDERBILT

11

PARK AVENUE

86TH STREET

89TH STREET

104TH STREET

106TH ST.

14

10

EAST RIVER

ROOSEVELT ISLAND

STATEN ISLAND

NEW JERSEY

MANHATTAN ISLAND

THE BRONX

BROOKLYN

QUEENS

W

S

N

E

LONG ISLAND

MIDTOWN AND UPPER MANHATTAN TOUR

10 KIPS BAY. After defeating Washington on Long Island, the British crossed the East River and landed on Manhattan at the foot of East 34th Street. From here they moved toward Murray Hill in pursuit of the retreating Americans.

11 MURRAY HILL. The British advance stopped at the Murray farm, where Mary Murray supposedly delayed them until the Americans could retreat to Harlem Heights. A plaque at 35th Street and Park Avenue marks the farm's site.

12 NATHAN HALE. A plaque at Vanderbilt Avenue and 44th Street marks the vicinity where the patriot spy spoke the famous words, "I only regret that I have but one life to lose for my country," and was then hanged by the British.

13 THE NEW-YORK HISTORICAL SOCIETY. This museum, at 77th Street and Central Park West, has exhibits related to New York in Revolutionary times, including fragments of the statue of King George III.

14 GRACIE MANSION. In 1776, the British set the home of Jacob Walton and the nearby fortifications on fire. Archibald Gracie built a house there in 1799, now the residence of the Mayor of New York, at 89th Street and East End Avenue.

15 MUSEUM OF THE CITY OF NEW YORK. At 104th Street and Fifth Avenue, the museum offers a wide display of New York history, including period rooms, costumes, and an audio-visual presentation of the city's history since 1524.

16 McGOWN'S PASS. About 50 feet into Central Park from the 106th Street and Fifth Avenue entrance was McGown's Pass, where the victorious Americans reentered New York in 1783. A paved area and a cannon mark the site.

17 HARLEM HEIGHTS. This important battle was fought near the Hudson River at West 120th Street. Here the outnumbered Americans forced the Redcoats to retreat, proving they could hold their own against the experienced British troops.

18 MORRIS-JUMEL MANSION. Located in Roger Morris Park at West 160th Street and Edgecombe Avenue, this home, built in 1765, served as Washington's headquarters during the Battle of Harlem Heights. It is open to the public.

NEW YORK TODAY